Botanical Art
TO CUT OUT AND
COLLAGE

OVER 500 BOTANICAL ILLUSTRATIONS
TO INSPIRE CREATIVITY

Royal Botanic Gardens Kew

DAVID & CHARLES

www.davidandcharles.com

CONTENTS

INTRODUCTION

BOTANICAL ART is as popular today as it has ever been, perhaps even more so, as we all realise the importance of connecting with nature in an increasingly fast-paced world. It has been scientifically proven that just looking at pictures of plants can have a calming effect on the mind, lowering stress levels and supporting relaxation. The same is true of making things by hand – away from screens and digital distractions – and so combining the traditional craft of collage with botanical art is an immensely mindful activity that will benefit all who have a go.

Plants have been represented in art for over 4000 years but the scientific use of botanical illustration to record and identify plant species is believed to have begun in Ancient Greece. A physician named Crateuas (111–64BCE) is widely thought to be the first documented scientific botanical artist – his illustrated *Rhizotomica* described the medicinal properties of numerous plants known to the Greeks.

The art form blossomed in the era of exploration – many early botanists were artists themselves, or hired an artist to accompany them on expeditions in the field, as sending specimens back home risked damage or decay. An artist was often the first to officially document many of the plants we know today. But even after the invention of photography, botanical illustration remained a crucial medium. Photography can't bring each unique detail of a plant to life; whereas an artist can hone in on the way a leaf is attached to a stem, the formation of spikelets or hidden features beyond what's in a photo. Photos can be deceptive but the job of the botanical artist is to capture absolute truth.

The Royal Botanic Gardens, Kew has never gone a day without an artist in its ranks, and modern-day science still relies on this ancient tradition. It is one of the most specific and vital art forms that plays a major part in botanical documentation. Every painting that a trained botanical artist creates becomes the visual definition of its subject. At Kew, this plate becomes cemented in history as part of a 200,000-strong botanical illustrative archive. Published alongside a written description, the artist's plate is part of the definition of a plant. They appear in journals, floras and field guides. One of the best examples is *Curtis's Botanical Magazine*, the world's longest running, illustrated botanical journal – a definitive publication on botany and horticulture, continuously published since 1787, produced by Kew to this day. Many of the images in this book have come from *Curtis's*, and it is remarkable to see that they are as fresh and engaging today as the day they were drawn.

Kew's collection is a working resource, used by Kew staff and visiting researchers as a reference tool, but as the art is appreciated by everyone, we hope that this book will bring it to a wider audience, who can engage with it on a more personal and purely aesthetic level, bringing some botanical beauty to art and craft projects in new and exciting ways.

HOW TO USE THIS BOOK

FEATURING OVER 500 images, this book presents a wide variety of botanical art across a range of chapters – from flowers to cacti, fruit and vegetables, and even fungi.

While we hope that you find this to be a beautiful book in itself, it is designed to be used and not kept on the shelf – cut it up, create beautiful art from it, and share your creations with the people you love, as well as with us by tagging @kewgardens and @dandcbooks when posting any of your makes to social media.

We have been careful to ensure that all the images in the book can be used, as the reverse side of each page is printed with a patterned paper, so you don't have to worry about choosing between one image or another. To avoid any waste, we would also encourage you to use any leftover scraps of patterned papers in your collage projects too. These can make great borders or tabs for journal pages, be used as trimmings on card-making projects, and in a myriad of other creative ways.

On the following pages, we have included various ideas for using the images in this book. But first, do be sure to follow the guidance here on different ways of cutting, composing and securing your collages.

Fussy Cutting – Use scissors or a craft knife to cut exactly around the outline of the image, with no background remaining.

Rough Cutting – Use scissors to cut-out the image, leaving a border of the background showing. This is useful when the image has very fine or thin details.

Tearing – Similar to rough cutting, tearing will leave a border of the background around the image, but with a softer effect. Tear carefully around the image by hand – very roughly at first – you can always tear away into the edges further to refine the shape.

TIP – When cutting, cut just inside the image – this will make sure there are no bits of the background showing.

Composition – Lay images, colours and backgrounds on your surface and move them around, adjusting, adding or taking away until the arrangement feels right. Experiment and don't start gluing until you are happy with the design.

Glue – A simple glue stick is inexpensive, easy-to-use and clean. These are ideal if you are only using paper to make your collage. If you are using a mixture of mediums such as paper, wood and fabric, then PVA glue will be the best choice and this can also be used for découpage. Alternatively, you could use a specialist découpage medium such as Mod Podge which is a good all-round option and acts as a glue, sealer and finish for your projects. For a strong and waterproof finish, an acrylic medium will give a professional result and is available in matte or gloss finishes.

CREATING COLLAGES

COLLAGING IMAGES together is a fun and therapeutic activity with a wide range of applications. The word 'collage' derives from the French verb *coller*, meaning 'to glue' or 'to stick'. We hope that the collection of images included in this book will give you endless inspiration for your collage projects. The suggestions that follow might kick-start your creativity but are intended only as suggestions, and you can use your own imagination to develop your own collage creations however you desire – cutting and sticking to your heart's content!

Fruity Gift Tag – Cut-out a circle of card and glue down a selection of leaf images until covered. Using sticky foam pads between layers to create a 3D effect, add various cut-out fruit images.

Floral Greetings Card – Using the patterned paper included, fold in half and draw half a heart against the fold - cut out and open to create a heart shape and glue to the centre of a card blank. Select and fussy cut a selection of flower and leaf designs. Starting with flower images with long stalks, create a symmetrical design on each side. Next, layer some leaf images towards the centre to continue the symmetrical pattern, and finally a group of flowers in the middle on the top layer.

Fabulous Fungi Tray – Paint a wooden tray with emulsion to create a strong background colour. Fussy cut your images - various sizes work best and lay out on the tray, starting at the top and working down in layers until you are happy with the arrangement. Put the images to one side and apply découpage medium or slightly watered down PVA glue to the surface of the tray and stick your images down following your layout, attaching small sections at a time. Apply a layer of découpage medium or slightly watered down PVA across the whole surface covering the design. To make the finished design hard wearing, apply a clear varnish over the whole tray.

Botanical Journal – Apply scrapbook paper (or make your own by ageing some lined paper) across the journal page. Fussy cut some floral designs (larger images work best) and glue coming in from the sides of the pages. Trim any excess from the edge with scissors. Line a small envelope with scrapbook paper (or a page from an old book) and glue down. You could also use the patterned pages in the book to create your own envelope. Use delicate flower designs (ones with long stems work best) to

place inside the envelope, only glue at the bottom so they create a 3D effect. You can also add some small sprigs of dried flowers into the envelope. Torn paper works well layered onto the page with items such as paper gift tags. Cut out or tear pieces of coloured paper to create spaces to write.

Antique Glass Frame – These frames are readily available and are an easy way to display a collaged scene. Cut out a few images and play around to get an attractive composition. Two or three larger floral stems work well. Remember you don't always need to use the whole image – cut off any extra stems or flowers if needed to fit the space, or add a single element like a butterfly. Lay your design down and close the frame to trap the collage in place. This means your arrangement can be changed regularly, perhaps with the seasons. If you are using smaller elements or want a permanent display, you can glue the images down.

Specimen Box Frame – Use a deep box/shadow frame to create a botanical specimen effect. Paint or cover the inside of your frame with paper to create a dark background - green, black or grey work well. Cut out individual images and attach using foam sticky pads to create a 3D effect. Cut out labels for each 'specimen' and use double-layered foam sticky pads to raise them above the plant images to finish the effect.

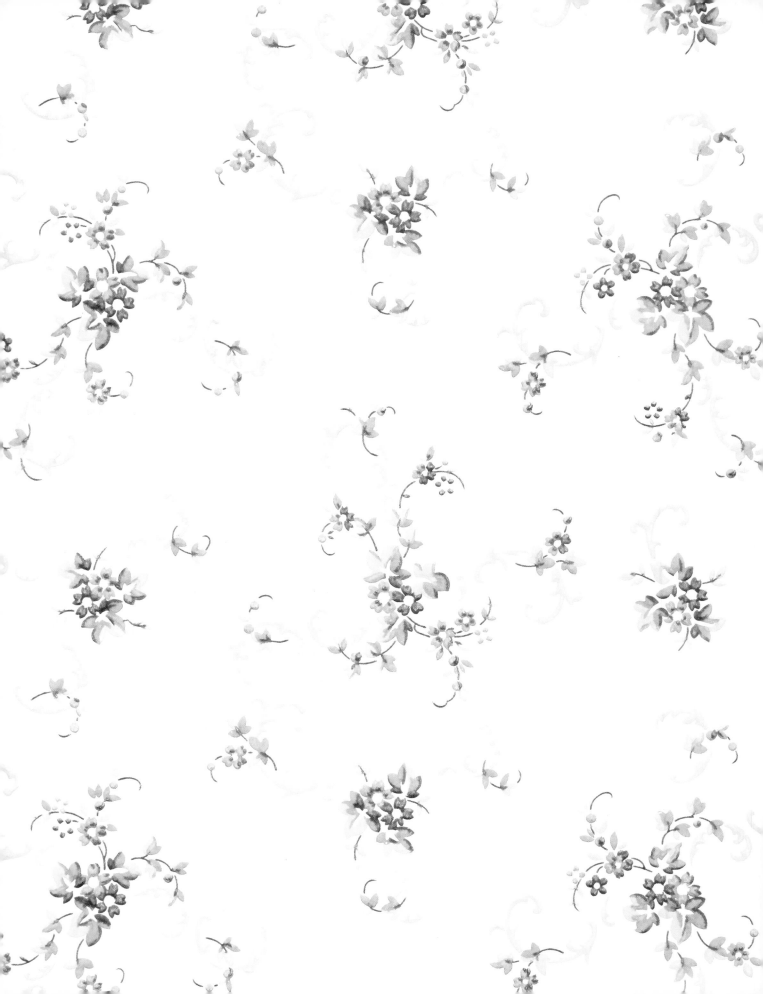

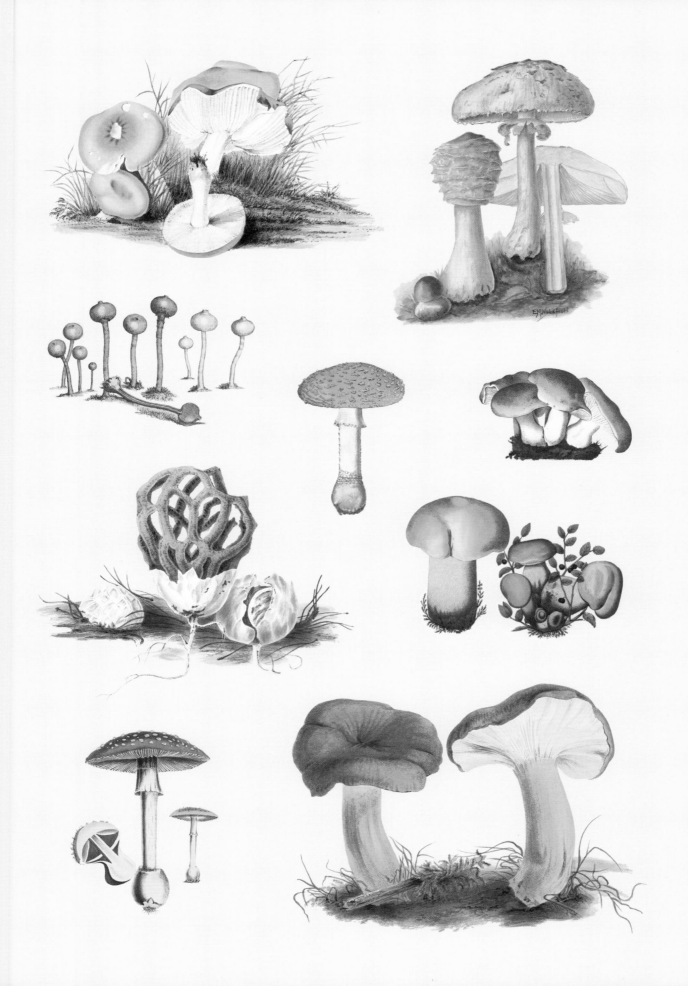

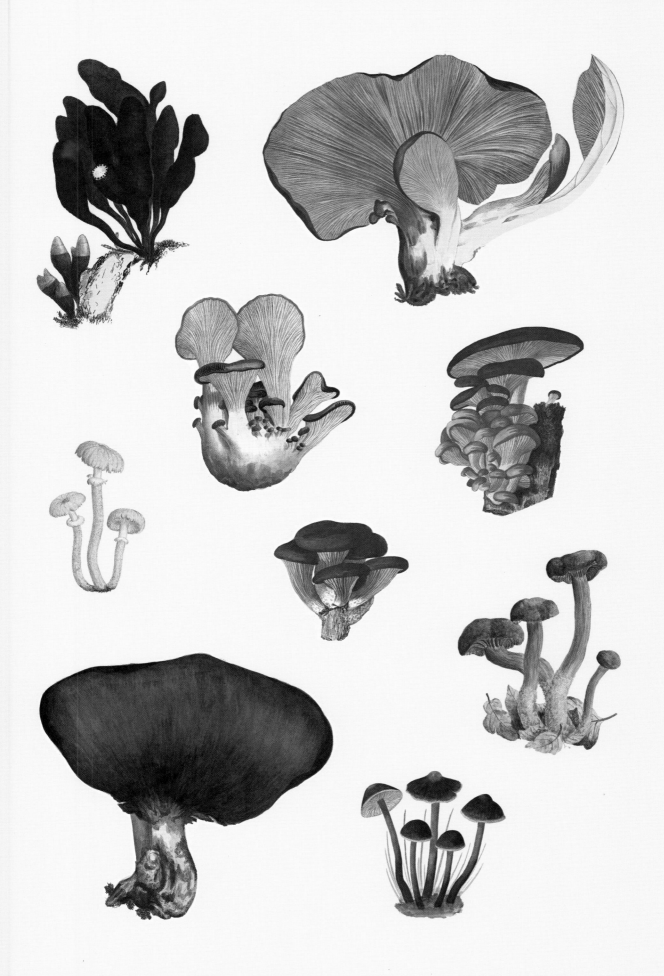

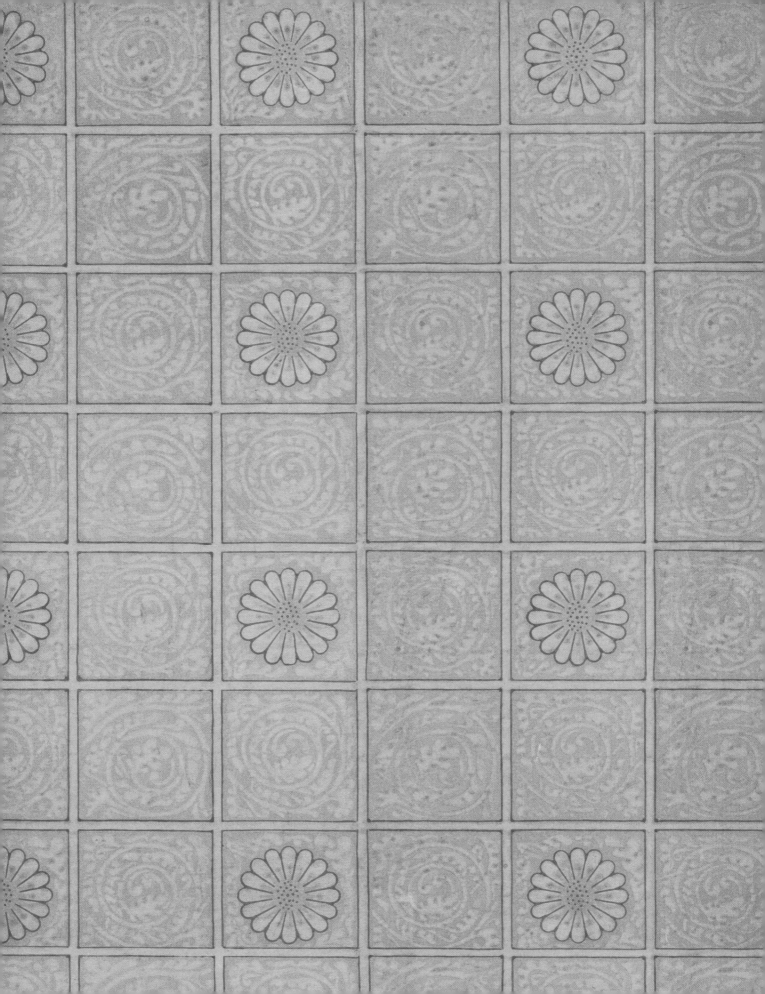

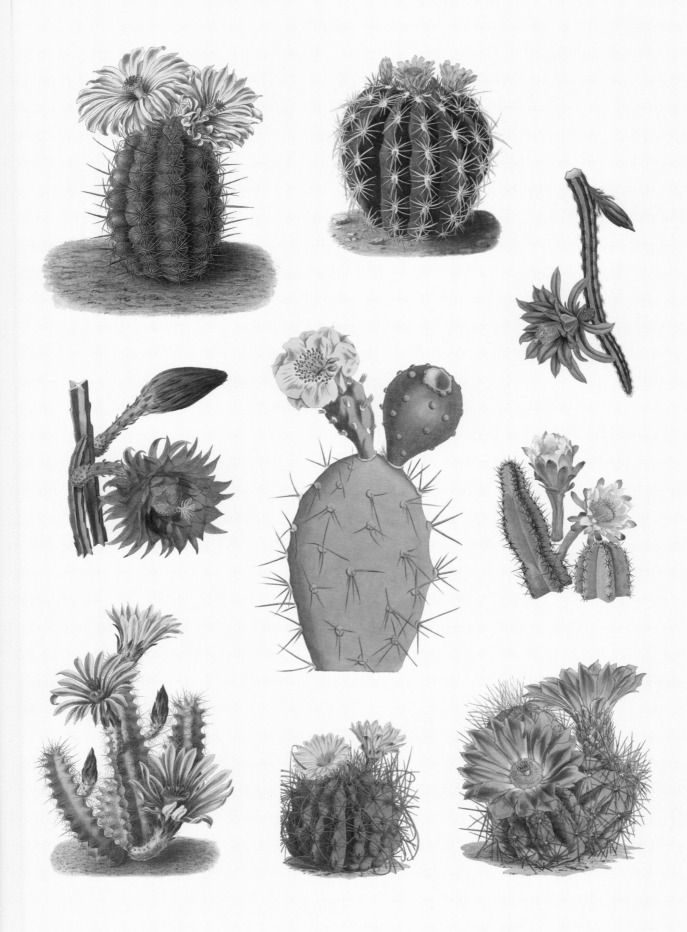

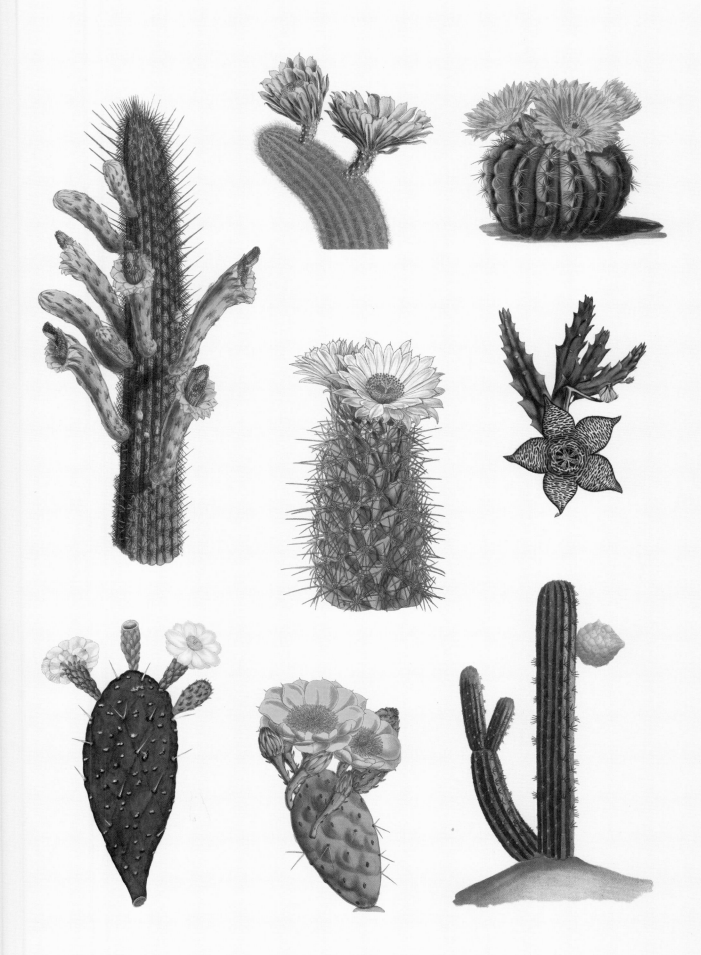

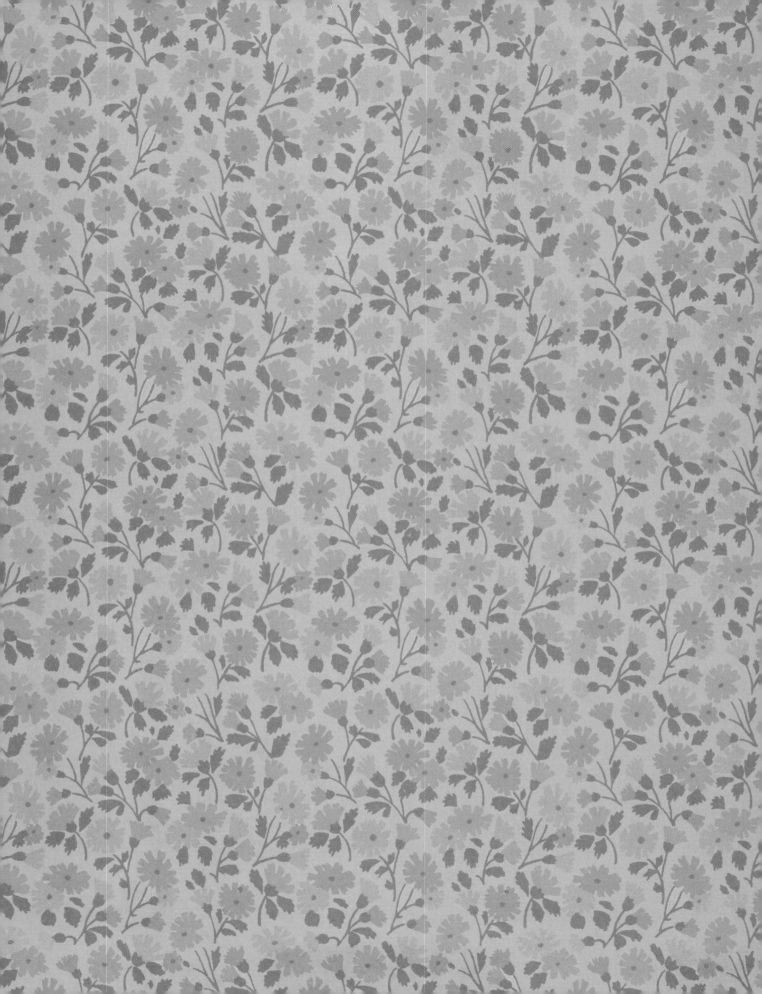

ABOUT KEW

THE ROYAL BOTANIC GARDENS, KEW is a world-famous research organisation and a major international visitor attraction. It is respected for its outstanding collections and scientific expertise in plant and fungal diversity, conservation, and sustainable development in the UK and around the globe. Kew's scientists and partners lead the way in the fight against biodiversity loss and finding nature-based solutions to the climate crisis. It harnesses the power of its science and the rich diversity of its gardens and collections to unearth why plants and fungi matter to everyone. It is fighting for a world where nature and biodiversity are understood, valued and protected.

Kew Gardens' 132 hectares of historic, landscaped gardens in London, and Kew's Wild Botanic Garden and 'living laboratory' in Wakehurst, Sussex, attract over 2.5 million visits every year. Kew Gardens was made a UNESCO World Heritage Site in July 2003 and celebrated its 260th anniversary in 2019.

Wakehurst is home to the Millennium Seed Bank, the largest wild plant seed bank in the world and a safeguard against the disastrous effects of climate change and biodiversity loss.

Kew holds one of the largest collections of botanical literature, art and archival material in the world. The library comprises 185,000 monographs and rare books, around 150,000 pamphlets, 5,000 serial titles and 25,000 maps. The archives contain vast collections relating to Kew's long history as a global centre of plant information and a nationally important botanic garden, including 7 million letters, lists, field notebooks, diaries and manuscript pages.

Kew receives approximately one third of its funding from Government through the Department for the Environment, Food and Rural Affairs (Defra) and research councils. Further funding needed to support Kew's vital work comes from donors, memberships and commercial activities including ticket sales.

For more information visit www.kew.org

A DAVID AND CHARLES BOOK
© David and Charles, Ltd 2023

David and Charles is an imprint of David and Charles, Ltd
Suite A, Tourism House, Pynes Hill, Exeter, EX2 5WS

Botanical Images © The Board of Trustees of the Royal Botanic Gardens, Kew 2023
Layout and Photography © David and Charles, Ltd 2023

First published in the UK and USA in 2023

A catalogue record for this book is available from the British Library.

ISBN-13: 9781446309933 paperback

This book has been printed on paper from approved suppliers and made from pulp from sustainable sources.

Printed in China through Asia Pacific Offset for:
David and Charles, Ltd
Suite A, Tourism House, Pynes Hill, Exeter, EX2 5WS

10 9 8 7 6 5 4 3 2 1

Publishing Director: Ame Verso
Managing Editor: Jeni Chown
Editor: Jessica Cropper
Head of Design: Anna Wade
Design and Art Direction: Prudence Rogers
Pre-press Designer: Ali Stark
Photography: Jason Jenkins
Production Manager: Beverley Richardson

David and Charles publishes high-quality books on a wide range of subjects.
For more information visit www.davidandcharles.com.

Share your makes with us on social media using #dandcbooks and follow us
on Facebook and Instagram by searching for @dandcbooks.